UNDERSTANDING THE FEAR OF THE LORD

The importance of walking in the light

Paul Halbeck

THE KINGDOM OF GOD IS NOT IN WORD BUT IN POWER
1st Corinthians 4:20
PowerMinistries.info
Partnering with the Alpha & Omega

UNDERSTANDING THE FEAR OF THE LORD

Unless otherwise indicated, all scripture quotations and search results have been taken from the King James Version (KJV) of the Bible.

All links and references within the text, point back to the ministry website: http://PowerMinistries.info

Copyright © 2019 by Paul Halbeck

All rights reserved. No part of this publication may be reproduced in its entirety for the purpose of making a profit. However, it is encouraged that you share the revelation you get from this book with others, for God's Word has been given to all and must remain freely available to all.

Understanding the Fear of the Lord,
the Importance of Walking in the Light.

Published by: PowerMinistries.info
ISBN Number: 978-1-7324676-1-3
Available from Amazon.com and other retail outlets.

Dedication

This book is dedicated to my Lord and Savior Jesus Christ and God's Holy Spirit, who over many years, has given me the revelation, wisdom and understanding as to what the fear of the Lord means and how to abide in this kingdom principle. The book was written for all who read it, that they might gain further insight into this very important concept, so that they might start growing in the wisdom and knowledge of the Lord; for the fear of the LORD is also the beginning of wisdom, Psalm 111:10.

I would also like to thank everybody that has made it possible, to bring the truth of God's Word out in book form; much thanks to my proofreaders, publisher, narrator, etc. May God bless you, as we all learn to walk in the light, as He is in the light, 1st John 1:7.

Table of Contents

Introduction: -------------------------------- 5

Understanding the Fear of the Lord: ----------- 11

    What the scriptures say: --------------- 13

    Man's vain philosophies: --------------- 25

    Similar NT. Scriptural Concerns: --------- 41

    Two Kingdoms, One Lawgiver: ----------- 51

How scripture defines evil: ------------------ 61

Our thoughts matter the most: --------------- 73

Closing Comments: ------------------------- 83

Introduction

Understanding and abiding in "the fear of the Lord" is an essential kingdom concept that we all need to understand. For walking in this concept is beneficial to both the believer and the unbeliever alike. However, the word "fear," in the phrase brings about many various emotions and has caused many people to either quickly justify it away or to ignore the concept altogether.

The world that we live in runs on various degrees of fear and likewise, most people are all too familiar with living under manageable levels of fear. We may use a different name such as "our stress level," but it really comes down to living under and being motivated by a degree of fear.

Therefore, since we are very familiar with living under certain levels of fear, it is all too easy for us to simply add God to our list of what or who we need to somehow fear. We generally do this to our own hurt, without further studying out the matter. We craft clever and vain philosophies as to what "the fear of the Lord," means, such as meaning a "healthy-fear," a "reverent-fear," or simply "being in awe."

Understanding the fear of the Lord

Abiding by "the fear of the Lord" is a kingdom principle and it is essential to know and understand this. In this book, you will learn what the scriptures say about "the fear of the Lord," and other similar scriptural concerns. I approach this from as many angles as possible, hence the reason for things that you might view as being redundancies.

Because we live in this dark world, most of us are trained that when we hear the word fear, we apply it directly and literally to ourselves. Believing that we are the recipient of something that we need to be cautious of, or somehow be scared of.

When we then apply it to our Lord, confusion sets in, and we start to wonder if we are to live all our days somehow fearing God our Creator, who blessed man in the garden. This would also be in contradiction when Jesus said to His disciples, "fear not." Likewise, when the people of the Bible had encounters with angels that told them not to fear.

For we realize that fear is not an attribute of God; rather, it is an attribute of the world or of the devil. However, from early on, we learn to be motivated by fear: i.e. (fear of death, fear of failure, fear of rejection from others and even from God, fear of heights), the list is almost endless.

Introduction

Having all this to deal with, now we are faced with thinking that we might need to somehow fear God too, it becomes just too much for us to handle. So, we generally either redefine the concept or just end up ignoring it altogether.

This book will make the kingdom concept of "the fear of the Lord" clear. Scripture tells us that: "The fear of the Lord" is the beginning of wisdom and understanding; it is clean enduring forever: and it is also for our own benefit. Also, Jesus, in His earthly ministry, operated under "the fear of the Lord."

We will look at all of these pieces and see how they all come together. For the concept of "the fear of the Lord" is a simple principle, yet we have made it so complex. So we have attempted to explain it away through man's vain philosophies. Disregarding the concept of righteousness versus unrighteousness, and ignoring the essential kingdom concept, making it into a biblical doctrine. As the below scripture tells us:

> Wherefore the Lord said, For as much as this people draw near *Me* with their mouth, and with their lips do honor Me, but have removed their heart far from Me, <u>and their fear toward Me is taught by the precept of men</u>: Isaiah 29:13.

Understanding the fear of the Lord

Knowing and understanding the concept of "the fear of the Lord" is an age-old principle that we even see in the earliest bible book of Job.

There was a man in the land of Uz, whose name *was* Job; and that man was perfect and upright, and <u>one that feared God, and eschewed evil</u>, Job 1:1.

This concept has not changed nor will it ever change. Job may not have known at the time, but he had learned a kingdom concept to hate evil and then to flee from evil, thus allowing one to then be able to walk in fellowship with Him in the light, 1st John 1:7.

This book first defines what the phrase "the fear of the Lord," means, by looking at the scripture references, pointing out what they say and don't say. For the definition of "the fear of the Lord," is only to hate and flee from evil, Proverbs 8:13. Showing also how this foundational concept perfectly aligns itself with scriptures and kingdom concepts for today.

Then addressed is the common but wrong teaching of "the fear of the Lord" that has led the body of Christ (the earthly church) astray to not placing an importance on the concept of hating evil and fleeing from evil. Thus, showing the reader that it is all about kingdom concepts, the kingdom of

Introduction

darkness versus the kingdom of light. All of these then pointing to the scriptural concept of walking in the light as He is in the light, 1st John 1:7.

Equivalent New Testament concerns are then covered, such as: "having the fear of God," and "having holy fear." Also looking at how the term "the wrath of God," aligns itself with this same principle. And ending that section with scripture accounts where the people or multitude were moved with emotional fear, after experiencing the supernatural and thus confusing this with the kingdom concept of the fear of the Lord which is hating evil and fleeing from evil.

Kingdom issues are then further expounded upon to give the reader an overall understanding and visualization of the earthly realm that we live in, emphasizing what Jesus said;

> Enter ye in at the strait gate: for wide *is* the gate, and broad *is* the way, that leads to destruction, . . . and narrow *is* the way, which leads unto life, Matthew 7:13-14.

Expounding then on the truth that God is the only Lawgiver, and how this also relates to the concept.

Understanding the fear of the Lord

Then to give this teaching a practical application of how we can position ourselves to abide in "the fear of the Lord." We take a look at how scripture defines what evil is. This all nicely comes together and gives us further understanding of how we can make it all happen and begin to walk in "the fear of the Lord."

Therefore, let us begin our study so we can reap all the benefits of abiding in the "fear of the Lord." It is my hope that this short book and teaching will give you a proper understanding of what, "the fear of the Lord" is. And you will then be able to grow in wisdom, understanding and your relationship with the Lord, Luke 2:52.

Understanding
the Fear of the Lord

The importance of walking in the light.

What the scriptures say:

Whenever we seek to understand a biblical concept, we must always be sure that we are building upon a correct foundation. Remaining consistent with other biblical truths, and the operation of God's kingdom. Therefore, I first establish these scriptures as a beginning foundation.

God is a Spirit of love (John 4:24), & (1st John 4:8)	And perfect love casts out fear, 1st John 4:18

From this, we can say: there is not any fear in God, and even being in Him will cast out fear. But wait, this no-fear zone also applies to us too.

For <u>God has not given us the spirit of fear</u>; but of power, and of love, and of a sound mind, 2nd Timothy 1:7.

Are we then to somehow fear a God of Love?

If man is in fear, it is either coming from the world's system or from the devil himself. If there were a reason for man to be in fear or to regard God or others with a certain fear, God would have given man a godly ability to fear; rather He told us that:

Understanding the fear of the Lord

> **Thou wilt keep** *him* **in perfect peace,** *whose* **mind** *is* **stayed** *on Thee:* **because he trusts in Thee,** Isaiah 26:3.

It is impossible to fully trust a person that we have reason to be in fear of or reason to regard with a certain fear. If we are seeking and trusting God, we will be in perfect peace. And if we reside in perfect peace, it's impossible to be in literal fear or to regard someone with a certain fearful concern.

At first sight, these foundational truths only seem to muddy up the waters since they do not even allow for one to be in any type of fear. So what does "the fear of the Lord," mean and why was it given such a scary name if no one is to get into fear? This will all come together for you as you read on.

The Bible always defines itself if we but seek out its truth, and the scripture definition is.

> **The fear of the LORD** *is* **to hate evil: pride, and arrogancy, and the evil way, and the froward mouth, do I hate,** Proverbs 8:13.

God loves righteousness and hates iniquity, (Hebrews 1:9, Zechariah 8:17, Psalm 97:10), and we must also learn to hate what He hates; simply doing this alone, will cause us to start walking in "the fear of the Lord."

What the scriptures say:

This definition may surprise you a bit because it does not talk about directly fearing or having a fearful concern towards the Lord; rather, it talks about hating the things that the Lord hates. As we continue with the teaching, this will all come together. We will then see it to be an essential and valid kingdom concept that we must follow rather than making a vain and clever philosophy out of it.

To clearly see the path to how we can abide in "the fear of the Lord." We need to know what all the scriptures say. Therefore, I have put together the scriptures in a logical progression of steps. Making the principle clear to see, showing you their purpose and then later how they can be applied.

First, we must depart from evil:

> By mercy and truth iniquity is purged: and by the fear of the LORD *men depart from evil*, Proverbs 16:6.
>
> The fear of the LORD *is* a fountain of life, to depart from the snares of death, Proverbs 14:27.
>
> And unto man he said, Behold, the fear of the Lord, that *is* wisdom; and to depart from evil *is* understanding, Job 28:28.

Understanding the fear of the Lord

Then we can begin to learn wisdom and gain a good understanding:

> The fear of the LORD *is* the instruction of wisdom; and before honor *is* humility. Proverbs 15:33.

> The fear of the LORD *is* the beginning of wisdom: a good understanding have all they that do *His commandments:* His praise endureth for ever. Psalm 111:10.

> The fear of the LORD *is* the beginning of wisdom: and the knowledge of the holy *is* understanding. Proverbs 9:10.

"The fear of the Lord" is the beginning of wisdom, knowledge and good understanding. Therefore, we cannot even begin to grow in these things until we learn this essential concept. For if we have not yet departed from the darkness, we cannot retain wisdom, knowledge, and understanding that is only found within the light.

Also know that these scriptural concepts will always be with us, for:

> The fear of the LORD *is* clean, enduring forever: the judgments of the LORD *are* true *and* righteous altogether, Psalm 19:9.

Within this scripture, we see that:

What the scriptures say:

1). **The fear of the Lord is not something to shun; it is <u>clean</u>**, it is to be desired and embraced as you would a clean white righteous garment, Revelations 19:8, having departed from living in unrighteousness and now walking in the light, as He is in the light, 1ˢᵗ John 1:7.

2). **The fear of the Lord <u>endures forever</u>**, the concept is valid for today and for all times, it was not canceled at the cross, nor will it go away when we get to heaven.

3). **The "fear of the Lord" has to do with <u>the LORD's righteous judgments</u>**. Thus, we see that He is judging between the righteous and the unrighteous.

Benefits of operating in the fear of the Lord:

By humility *and* the fear of the LORD *are* <u>riches, and honor, and life</u>, Proverbs 22:4.

The fear of the LORD *is* <u>a fountain of life</u>, to depart from the snares of death, Proverbs 14:27.

The fear of the LORD <u>prolongs days</u>: but the years of the wicked shall be shortened, Proverbs 10:27.

The fear of the LORD <u>*tends* to life</u>: and *he that has it* shall abide satisfied; he shall not be visited with evil, Proverbs 19:23.

These scriptures show us that knowing and abiding in "the fear of the Lord" is a good thing. It brings riches and is a fountain of life that prolongs your days and satisfies your life. If it were something to be afraid of or to be regarded with a fearful concern, it would create stress, shorten your days, and would lead to sickness and death.

Our New Testament example.

> Then had the churches rest throughout all Judea and Galilee and Samaria, and were edified; and <u>walking in the fear of the Lord</u>, and in the comfort of the Holy Ghost, were multiplied, Acts 9:31.

The New Testament church walked in "the fear of the Lord," showing us that it applies to us today. And as we have seen in Psalm 19:9, the principle will endure forever, so we had best learn this concept now while we are here on this earth.

This exact phrase, "the fear of the Lord," is found 27 times in the Bible, 26 times in the Old Testament and one time in the New Testament. Although this is mostly an Old Testament term, there are similar New Testament scriptural concerns that we will also cover later on.

What the scriptures say:

What scripture has shown us so far:

So far, we have seen that "the fear of the Lord" is the principle of hating evil and departing from evil. It is the beginning of wisdom, it is clean and endures forever. Lending itself towards a fruitful, fulfilled and a long life.

You might be thinking this is a bit incomplete, wondering where the fear God part comes in. I will address this and other issues. However, I first want to emphasize what the scriptures tell us, and also letting it become evident what they do not say.

Seek the Lord and He will teach you.

> [8] O taste and see that the LORD *is* good: blessed *is* the man *that* trusts in Him. [9] O fear the LORD, ye His saints: for *there is* no want to them that fear Him. [10] The young lions do lack, and suffer hunger: but they that seek the LORD shall not want any good *thing*. [11] Come, ye children, <u>hearken unto me: I will teach you the fear of the LORD</u>. Psalm 34:8-11.

Here we see that "the fear of the Lord" is a concept that needs to be learned. Learning first requires having a desire, followed by giving of the time, effort and perseverance to see it through.

Understanding the fear of the Lord

We must seek out the truth:

Seeking out the truth of the scripture requires effort on our part. Although salvation is a gift to all that confess Jesus and believe that God raised Him from the dead, Romans 10:9, gaining wisdom and knowledge requires study, time and persistence.

Scripture tells us that we must desire wisdom more than silver or gold. Thus, we must prize getting wisdom from above, more than we do our earthly treasures. In this life, we put great effort, time and planning into obtaining our worldly possessions. In general, we also need to do the same to achieve Godly wisdom. This pleases God, for it is His desire that all of us would grow in the wisdom, knowledge and the understanding of His kingdom.

Seeking out the things of God's kingdom was never meant to be hidden from us, but rather hidden for us. So that when we finally put forth the time and effort required to learn and understand them, we will see these biblical truths and concepts that we have learned as being far more valuable than silver and gold, Proverbs 16:16.

> *It is* the glory of God to conceal a thing: but the honor of kings *is* to search out a matter, Proverbs 25:7.

What the scriptures say:

If thou seeks her as silver, *{wisdom}* and searches for her as *for* hid treasures; ⁵ Then shalt thou understand the fear of the LORD and find the knowledge of God, Proverbs 2:4-5

Better *is* little with the fear of the LORD than great treasure and trouble therewith, Proverbs 15:16.

The principle of "the fear of the Lord" is always connected to wisdom.

For that they hated knowledge, and did not choose the fear of the LORD, Proverbs 1:29

The fear of the LORD *is* the beginning of knowledge: *but* fools despise wisdom and instruction, Proverbs 1:7.

And wisdom and knowledge shall be the stability of thy times, *and* strength of salvation: the fear of the LORD *is* his treasure, Isaiah 33:6.

The importance of hating evil is also an Old Testament concept.

Ye that love the LORD, hate evil: He preserves the souls of His saints; He delivers them out of the hand of the wicked, Psalm 97:10.

We must learn from O.T. scriptures

Scripture tells us that ALL scripture is profitable for correction and instruction, 2nd Timothy 3:16, and that Old Testament scriptures were written for our learning, Romans 15:4. Knowing that the Word does not change, we therefore need to learn from and apply this foundational concept of hating evil and fleeing from evil to other scriptures of like concern.

Later on in the book, we will see how the principles of hating the darkness and fleeing from it (evil), also perfectly apply to New Testament scriptures. And through doing so, it provides us with more clarity to build upon. For scripture tells us that we need to build precept upon precept, line upon line, here a little, *and* there a little: Isaiah 28:10.

A much more positive approach:

Abiding in "the fear of the Lord" can be likened to walking in the light, 1st John 1:7. Walking in righteousness and having a fear of living in unrighteousness. For living unrighteously can distract us from ever seeking God's kingdom, being overtaken by unrighteous ways and possibly even leading to our own eternal destruction.

What the scriptures say:

Points to Ponder:
What the scriptures say:
- It's all about hating what God hates. He hates unrighteousness and does not want His people to walk in darkness, for doing so allows the enemy to harm us and can also lead to eternal damnation.
- Go with what the Bible says: it defines "the fear of the Lord" as hating evil, Proverbs 8:13. Don't add man's clever reasonings to it.
- Scripture tells us, "The fear of the Lord" is the beginning of wisdom and good understanding. Therefore, before we can even start to learn and retain godly wisdom that can only be found in the light, we must comply with this concept.
- Abiding in "the fear of the Lord," will always result in walking in the light, as He is in the light, 1ˢᵗ John 1:7. This will be further emphasized later on.
- Praise God, for He is good! He blessed man at creation, and He has good thoughts and plans for man. Also, we are to be one with Him, and that pretty much rules out any concept of fear, whether it be literal or figurative toward God, our Creator right there.

Man's vain philosophies:

Because the phrase "the fear of the Lord" sounds rather intimidating. Thus, throughout the centuries, people have rushed in to define the phrase and to negate any fearful thoughts or concerns that they might have. This has happened for a few different reasons, from ignorance or genuinely being confused, to deliberately choosing to look the other way. However, before we start addressing man's vain philosophies, we need to understand why men have chosen to place their clever reasonings over certain biblical and kingdom truths.

Fundamentally, it's all about what kingdom we choose to believe in and partake of, the kingdom of light or the kingdom of darkness with its many shades of gray. We can think of these kingdoms as being on the same spectrum.

Even though we live in this dark physical world that has several shades of gray, we can still partake of the kingdom of light. For it is not about what kingdom we physically abide in. It is about what kingdom we choose to believe in and partake of.

Understanding the fear of the Lord

Luke 17:21 tells us that the kingdom of God is within us. It is our choice; either we can partake of God's kingdom within us, believing in it by faith along with agreeing with the truth of God's Word; or we can believe in the world's system, what we experience through our natural senses, and living according to all the facts and statistics that the world hands us. But, we cannot believe in some of both; that option has not been left open to us.

> No servant can serve two masters: for either he will hate the one, and love the other; or else he will hold to the one, and despise the other. Ye cannot serve God and mammon, Luke 16:13.

What generally hinders us is that we do not see this world as a dark place, and we certainly do not view most of our actions as less than righteous. I believe this is the main reason why we place certain of our reasonings over biblical truths. For we would rather justify our darkened, fallen world than see it and our actions for what they really are. Therefore, we redefine what God calls darkness, allowing us to minimize and perhaps even nullify the concept of hating evil and fleeing from it.

> The world cannot hate you; but Me it hates, because I testify of it, that the works thereof are evil, John 7:7.

Man's vain philosophies:

Jesus spoke this to His brothers, and I am sure when the Pharisees heard of it, it did not go over well with them. Most likely, it also became one of the reasons they also wanted to kill Him. For the Pharisees and the religious leaders of the day, most likely saw themselves as clean and upright. They did not want anyone telling them that the ways of the world that they lived in were evil, thus imparting to them that their ways were also less than righteous.

This same reasoning also applies to us today. For this world can be cold, uncaring and even a cruel place, while even at its best this world is quite less than utopia. But since this world and its ways are primarily all that we know and are familiar with, we attempt to justify the darkness. For our flesh and the unrenewed man actually enjoys, (scripture even says 'loved') the darkness, John 3:19. Therefore, if our mind is not renewed to the new man, rather than acknowledging the world as a dark and fallen place that it is, we attempt to sanitize the darkness. As scripture says, we start calling what is evil – good, and what is good - evil.

> Woe unto them that call evil good, and good evil; that put darkness for light, and light for darkness; that put bitter for sweet, and sweet for bitter! Isaiah 5:20.

Understanding the fear of the Lord

And this is the condemnation, that light is come into the world, and men loved darkness rather than light, because their deeds were evil, John 3:19.

Thus, we tend to find ways to justify our unrighteous acts, putting our clever reasonings and philosophies over biblical truths because:

1). **It makes us feel better about ourselves.** As we convince ourselves that we are upright and are near pure in heart, as we remain in our unrighteous lifestyle and our immorality.

2). **It frees us from being responsible to a Holy God.** Else, we would need to humble ourselves and submit to a righteous and holy God and learn His righteous ways. Repenting of our sins and leaving some of our known earthly ways and pleasures behind us.

These reasons are by no means new; people have used clever reasonings throughout the centuries to legitimize living in the darkness and certain sins. Thus, coming up with various vain philosophies that either negate or minimize the concept of hating and fleeing from evil. As we see in the below scripture, Isaiah is prophesying not only that the people give the Lord lip service, but also the reason why.

Man's vain philosophies:

Wherefore the Lord said, For as much as this people draw near Me with their mouth, and with their lips do honor Me, but have removed their heart far from Me, <u>and their fear toward Me is taught by the precept of men</u>: Isaiah 29:13.

A misleading term called "reverential-fear."

The most widely used reasoning to explain away what "the fear of the Lord" is, is what people call "reverential-fear." By coining this word combination, people are attempting to neutralize the word "fear," redefining it to be more or less a "healthy-fear." Within this fallen world that we live in, this does have a certain twisted logic to it, i.e. "you need to look both ways before crossing a street; otherwise a car or truck might mow you down."

When we casually define the phrase as simply using a "respectful-fear," or a "healthy-caution," we have purposely defined a concept that we can easily deal with. However, we have also unknowingly hindered our spiritual growth and walk in Christ, for this puts a distance between us and God. God is not about to mow us down; the plans and thoughts that He has for us, are good and not of evil, Jeremiah 29:11. However, our flesh and the unrenewed man actually prefers it this way, for we have negated the true concept of hating and fleeing from the darkness. Allowing us to remain in our unrighteous ways, while also believing that we are genuinely abiding in the "fear of the Lord."

Now before going any further, let me say that I am not against reverencing God, I am all for giving God reverence, honor, worship and praise and likewise, every believer should also do so. My point is that reverence is not part of the definition of abiding in "the fear of the Lord." In fact, if you consider reverencing God as fulfilling "the fear of the Lord," you have turned a blind eye to the harm of what walking in darkness can do to you. And you have also minimized or negated the concept of walking in the light, as He is in the light, 1st John 1:7.

Whereby, every Christian should reverence the Lord; reverence will not teach you how to hate and flee from evil and how to walk in the light with Him, as He is in the light. Once we learn to do these things, we will then naturally give Him pure worship and reverence, as we will then be walking in the light in fellowship with Him. Rather than just praising Him with our flesh and giving Him lip-service, as we continue to walk in our unrighteous ways.

Man's vain philosophies:

Reverential-fear is what I call a "user obscured definition," for it provides the user with two contradictory terms, (reverence and fear). Requiring the user to self-define the phrase and also the required action to achieve the desired end result. Allowing one to assume, that if they reverence God long enough or hard enough or even say to God in prayer that they reverence Him, they will be abiding in "the fear of the Lord." Whereas walking in "the fear of the Lord" will naturally result in reverence for God, we cannot get there through the action of reverence. For we cannot claim an end result unless we first apply the concept that allows us to achieve it.

We can better understand how we cannot claim an end result until we perform its required concept by looking at the gift of salvation. Our salvation from eternal damnation should also result in reverence for God. However, the only way we become saved is to confess that Jesus is the Son of God and believe that God raised Him from the dead, Romans 10:9.

Reverencing God without believing and confessing will not bring about salvation. An unbeliever that reverences and praises God due to their circumstance of good fortune, yet refusing to believe in Jesus, and that God raised Him from the dead, remains an unbeliever. Likewise, we cannot put reverence before we understand and walk in, the concept and constraints of "the fear of the Lord." By doing this, we actually nullify the importance of hating unrighteousness and walking in the light.

How people have attempted to reason the phrase "reverential-fear":

1. **By overlaying N.T. scripture on top of O.T. scriptures.** People use the reasoning that Jesus not only equated the next two scriptures, but also substituted and replaced the phrase "fear the LORD thy God," with the phrase "worship the Lord thy God."

Thou shalt fear the LORD thy God, and serve Him, and shalt swear by His name, Deuteronomy 6:13, {10:12, 10:20, 13:4}.

Then said Jesus unto him, Get thee hence, Satan: for it is written, Thou shalt worship the Lord thy God, and Him only shalt thou serve, Matthew 4:10, {Luke 4:8}.

Making this change implies that N.T. Scripture concepts can replace what O.T. scriptures say. This is nothing less than revising scripture to serve one's own purpose. For Jesus Christ, the Word made flesh,

Man's vain philosophies:

is the same yesterday, today and forever. Since we do not know of an exact word for word match of the Words Jesus spoke, we could also index His Words to other Old Testament scriptures that do speak about worshiping the Lord, i.e. "thou shalt worship no other god: for the LORD, whose name *is* Jealous, *is* a jealous God:", Exodus 34:14.

In Old Testament times, the people did not have all of the teachings that we now have in the New Testament. We have the Gospels and teachings of Jesus, the Epistles, and the book of Revelation, that all speak of the conflict between the two kingdoms of light and darkness. With the limited understanding that the people had in Old Testament times, a directly communicated fear of God was perhaps the best way to get the message across.

However, now under the New Testament, we are not under a schoolmaster, but under a higher way, and the teachings of the Epistles. My point is that we are to increase in knowledge, Ephesians 1:17. Being not babes in Christ, but able to be fed with the meat of the Word, 1st Corinthians 3:1. Hence, "The fear of the Lord" is a concept that has never changed and we need to seek out and understand the importance of hating and fleeing from evil.

Understanding the fear of the Lord

<u>⁴ If thou seeks her</u> *(wisdom, understanding & knowledge)*, <u>as silver, and searches for her as</u> *for* <u>hid treasures;</u> ⁵ <u>Then shalt thou understand the fear of the LORD, and find the knowledge of God</u>, Proverbs 2:4-5.

Another way people have reasoned what "the fear of the Lord," means is:

2. **By adding to word definitions.**

Determining what "the fear of the Lord," means, has been an issue down through the centuries. To the extent that most modern-day dictionaries now have a separate definition just to include "reverential-fear." Some of the modern-day Bible translations also have started using the term "reverential-fear," as does Strong's Concordance that was written many years back, also has such an entry.

The Greek word ***phobeo*** Strong's #5399, used in the New Testament is defined and has been used as meaning either:

1). *to frighten,*
2). *to be in awe of,*
3). *to be afraid, or*
4). *to fear with (exceedingly) reverence.*

This Greek word has been used in scriptures as any of these four definitions. Click here for a detailed look at how the word has been used.

Man's vain philosophies:

This allows the user to self-define the concept any way they wish. And usually, we end up defining the word to agree with our own worldly logic, rather than taking the time to study out the scriptures and seek out the biblical concept.

I believe, most people choose to believe the false concept of "reverential-fear," for two main reasons;

- Because they know it does not make sense to fear God, and this is a convenient alternative.
- They do not wish to change their lifestyle, even though it may clearly be unrighteous.

Thus, they use this as a way to justify and convince themselves that they are abiding in "the fear of the Lord," even if it is to their own deception.

Two separate terms, reverence & fear:

In the scriptures that we have gone over, we have seen that reverence is not part of the definition. The only scripture that mentions both reverence and fear in the same verse, the terms are not combined. They are treated as two distinct terms separated by the conjunction "and."

> Wherefore we receiving a kingdom which cannot be moved, let us have grace, whereby we may serve God acceptably with reverence <u>and</u> godly fear: Hebrews 12:28.

The harm of the term "reverential-fear"

1). **It sets up a barrier between us and God.** For we then regard God with a certain fearful concern. Rather, God wishes for us to be in right relationship with Him, to fellowship with Him and to be one in Him.

2). **It negates the concept of hating and fleeing from evil.** It allows people to deceive themselves, thinking they are abiding by "the fear of the Lord," as they remain in and justify their unrighteous lifestyle.

3). **It keeps us from ever growing in the Lord.** We can only grow in Christ when we are walking in the light. For we cannot learn, retain and practice righteousness when we are walking in the darkness.

A last Analogy:

Believing "the fear of the Lord" is reverence towards God, can be compared to a man who committed a murder. And as he goes before the judge, his plan is to tell the righteous and just judge how much he honors, respects and reverences him, somehow thinking that this will get him off.

Man's vain philosophies:

Although the righteous judge might be pleased, puzzled, amused, or even put-off by this, it will not change what the man had done, the outcome of the case or the man's sentence.

For all who are in Christ Jesus, we have the gift of repentance that will change this outcome, but reverence won't. For God the Father is a righteous and just Judge and will condemn the unrighteous, even if it be His own creation. Trusting in the finished work of Jesus Christ and repenting of our sin is the only thing that will bring us back into a right relationship with God the Father. And all of us need to repent of our sinful deeds, for all of us one day will undergo such a judgment.

Now, back to our analogy of the man who committed the crime; The only way that the man could escape the judgment and the just sentencing of a righteous and just judge was to have never have committed the crime in the first place. Hence, he needed to be in fear of getting caught up in an unrighteous lifestyle that caused him to commit the murder that he did. What he needed to do was to walk in the light and shun the darkness. Rather than trying to placate and flatter the righteous judge by telling him that he reverenced him.

Understanding the fear of the Lord

Considering "the fear of the Lord," to be "awe or wonderment."

Believing this goes to the extreme of completely ignoring any personal responsibility of any kind.

> And the spirit of the LORD shall rest upon Him, the spirit of wisdom and understanding, the spirit of counsel and might, <u>the spirit of knowledge and of the fear of the LORD</u>; Isaiah 11:2.

This scripture tells us that the spirit of knowledge and of the fear of the Lord was upon our Lord Jesus. Knowing that Jesus came from His Father and was one with God, His Father, John 16:28. And that while Jesus was with us in His earthly ministry, He taught the people and did the supernatural works that His Father gave Him to finish, John 3:6. It just does not make sense that Jesus would be in awe of or be amazed by the kingdom works and miracles that His Father gave Him to do, and that He carried out.

Whereby, we might be amazed at aspects of the supernatural, I assure you that Jesus was not. Jesus expected blind eyes to be opened, the deaf to hear, the lame to walk and even the dead to be raised, and so should we, since we are to be His followers.

Man's vain philosophies:

We need to become so immersed in the Word that we believe and expect those things also to happen. Thus if we are amazed at the supernatural, it only speaks to us of just how hard our heart is due to unbelief in the supernatural, actually telling us of the overriding belief of the world ways we have within ourself.

For, this same anointing and power have been made available to us as scripture tells us that we have the full inheritance of Christ, Colossians 1:12. Also, Jesus told His disciples that if they believed on Him, they would do the works that He did and even greater works would they do, John 14:12.

Also, when we believe that "the fear of the Lord," translates into awe or wonderment. What we have once again done, perhaps without even realizing it, is we have put a distance between us and God. We might even view this as a proper and respectful thing, such as thinking that: "We being just a lowly sheep, are so amazed and awestruck by the mighty power of the Master."

As long as we live in this world, we may always, to some degree be amazed at the supernatural. However, know that awe and or wonderment plays no part in abiding in "the fear of the Lord."

Points to Ponder:
Man's vain philosophies:

- Remain open to biblical correction from the Word, 2nd Timothy 3:16. If you can see a truth in God's Word that you have not noticed before or have been taught contrary to, God's truth must always trump man's vain philosophies.

- The concept of "the fear of the Lord," has not changed over the years and it is wrong for man to cleverly redefine it. Jesus Christ (the Word made flesh), is the same yesterday, today, and forever, Hebrews 13:8.

- According to Proverbs 2:4-5, to know "the fear of the Lord," we need to seek for wisdom, and understanding as one would seek for silver and hidden treasures. This calls for us to put effort into it and to also be in a relationship with the Holy Spirit as we study the Word out for ourselves.

- Praise God; we never need to be at a loss at what God's Word means, for the Word can define itself. All that is required is the desire, time, effort and diligence to pursue the truth of the Word, Acts 17:11.

Similar NT. Scriptural Concerns:

The concept of "the fear of the Lord," applies to us today; it has not changed over the ages. However, now under the New Covenant and New Testament teachings, we need to understand the concept of "the fear of the Lord," rather than simply applying a direct fear towards God. Thus, as New Testament believers, we need to learn and progress in our understanding of God's Word beyond what was commonly known in the Old Testament period.

It was the Apostles Paul's desire in Hebrews chapter six, that believers would advance beyond the basic foundational doctrines of Christ and go on to perfection. Not needing to be fed again with the milk of the Word, but rather with meat. As we, therefore, progress in the revelation of the Word, we need to bring forth every scriptural truth that we have learned both old and new, Matthew 13:52.

The only way to advance in our doctrines of Christ is to apply the fundamental kingdom concept of hating evil and fleeing from evil. Then we will understand, retain and operate in righteous and Godly wisdom, as we walk in fellowship with Him, as He is in the light.

Understanding the fear of the Lord

In this part of the study, we will look at equivalent New Testament phrases, such as: "in the fear of God," "having a godly fear," as well as "the wrath of God," and addressing other scriptural concerns.

Equivalent New Testament terms.

"In the fear of God."

The phrase "in the fear of God," I see as having the same foundational meaning as "the fear of the Lord," of hating and fleeing from evil. Yet the scripture here provides us with further insight into what abiding in "the fear of the Lord," will do for us.

> Having therefore, these promises, dearly beloved, let us cleanse ourselves from all filthiness of the flesh and spirit, perfecting holiness in the fear of God, 2nd Corinthians 7:1.

The scripture tells us that the believer can perfect holiness through the fear of God. If we therefore, define attributes of what holiness is and how we can achieve it. Doing this will then tell us how we can also achieve and start walking in the fear of the Lord. Thus, I have listed a few attributes that define the words, "holy" or "holiness":

Similar NT. Scriptural Concerns:

Holiness: sanctified, righteous, consecrated., to be of moral, ethical, wholeness or of perfection,

The only way for someone to achieve these above qualities requires making an inward change and to be walking in the light. Reverence or awe or any other outward expression or admiration towards another just won't produce these qualities. Thus, this scripture also points us back to the definition of hating evil and fleeing from evil.

This scripture first talks about kingdom promises that are only available to us if we are walking in the light. Therefore, this also shows us that we must escape the darkness (evil), and be in the light to achieve the fullness of God's blessing and promises.

"With godly fear."

Wherefore we receiving a kingdom which cannot be moved, let us have grace, whereby we may serve God acceptably with reverence and godly fear: Hebrews 12:28.

In this scripture as we saw before, "reverence and godly fear," are two separate terms. Thus, if the scripture tells us to reverence God, then the meaning of "godly fear" must be different. Let me suggest here that godly fear is to be fearful of slipping back into a lifestyle of unrighteousness, that can distract us and can ultimately destroy us if we don't come out of it. For then the righteous Lawgiver would have to judge that person to eternal damnation.

"The wrath of God."

"The wrath of the Lord," is generally associated with the judgment on the last day. This is for unbelievers, for believers are called righteous as they abide in Christ Jesus and in His righteousness.

This is a judgment between righteousness and unrighteousness. And abiding in "the fear of the Lord" (departing from evil and walking in righteousness), is the principle that will keep us from the Lord's wrath. For, God does not wish that His righteous judgment should come upon any of us; He wishes that not one of us should perish.

> The Lord is not slack concerning His promise, as some men count slackness; but is longsuffering to us-ward, not willing that any should perish, but that all should come to repentance, 2nd Peter 3:9.

> For God has not appointed us to wrath, but to obtain salvation by our Lord Jesus Christ, 1st Thessalonians 5:9.

Similar NT. Scriptural Concerns:

For the wrath of God is revealed from heaven against all ungodliness and unrighteousness of men, who hold the truth in unrighteousness, Romans 1:18.

Let no man deceive you with vain words: for because of these things comes the wrath of God upon the children of disobedience, Ephesians 3:6.

All of the scriptures that we have looked at so far have been instructional regarding "the fear of the Lord." Telling of the underlining principle of hating evil and fleeing from evil, thus allowing one to then walk in the light with Christ, 1st John 1:7.

The next three classifications of scriptures and or accounts do not exactly fall into this category. I have included them, so as not to appear to have left out any scriptures or accounts that appear to be addressing a certain fearful concern.

The scriptures or accounts that we will close this section with; The first presents to us a severe warning message, whereas the second makes it clear to us that we always need to remain humble, ending with man's ever-changing emotions regarding how he perceives supernatural events.

Understanding the fear of the Lord

A harsh warning that there can be no wavering:

This account tells us of the consequences of what going back into the ways of the world can be, after you have been abiding under the Holy Spirit and His righteous power. The account of Ananias and Sapphira is as such. They sold a property and both, scheming together, held back part of the price, tempting and lying to the Spirit of the Lord. Thus, both fell down dead and great fear came upon all the church, as many that heard of this. You can read the entire account in Acts 5:1-10.

> And Ananias hearing these words fell down, and gave up the ghost: and great fear came on all them that heard these things. Acts 5:5.

When this took place, the early church was operating powerfully in the Holy Spirit, for the sick were healed even as Peter's shadow fell upon them. Thus, there was purity within the church that allowed God's Spirit to powerfully move among His people. Thus, when Ananias and Sapphira attempted to bring in some of the unrighteous, scheming and greedy ways of the world into the church. The pure and righteous power of God's Holy Spirit that was operating among them was compelled to condemn all unrighteousness.

Similar NT. Scriptural Concerns:

Please understand that it was not an angry God taking out His vengeance on a backslider. Rather it is that once we step into the light and start operating in the righteous power of the Holy Spirit, all darkness and unrighteous deeds become exposed and overcome by the light. For as we get closer to the true light and the glorious power within that light, stepping or slipping back into your worldly and unrighteous ways is a very dangerous thing to do. We cannot remain double-minded; that option is not open to us. The closer we get to the light; our focus must remain all the more steadfast on God's kingdom, His Son and abiding in His righteousness. Jesus conveyed to us in the scripture below that once we enter into the kingdom, our focus must remain entirely directed on pursuing the kingdom.

> [61] **And another also said, Lord, I will follow thee; but let me first go bid them farewell, which are at home at my house. [62] And Jesus said unto him,** No man, having put his hand to the plough, and looking back, is fit for the kingdom of God, Luke 9:61-62.

Scriptures emphasizing the Lord's holiness:

These scriptures emphasize the vast holiness of the Lord, related to us living in this fallen and darkened world. The two scriptures below were given to all of us as warning scriptures. We should not dismiss these scriptures once we become born-again and new creatures in Christ. But rather realize that the degree of fear that we will experience is directly proportional to the personal darkness that we walk in.

> *It is* a fearful thing to fall into the hands of the living God, Hebrews 10:31.
>
> And if the righteous scarcely be saved, where shall the ungodly and the sinner appear? 1st Peter 4:18.

Thus, yet another reason that we need to seek the light and flee from the darkness. That we should walk humbly and not count ourselves as more highly as we ought, Romans 12:3.

Reactions to amazing supernatural miracles:

We close with scriptures where the people, after seeing supernatural miracles, were amazed to the point of being in fear. There are many reactions to the supernatural, and generally, they are all driven by our emotions of fear and amazement. Fear of experiencing a power greater than what we are comfortable with, and amazement of what we cannot logically explain.

Similar NT. Scriptural Concerns:

However, know that the degree of fear that we experience from witnessing supernatural miracles or events is always inversely proportional to our relationship with God. For the more we cultivate our relationship and trust with a supernatural God, realizing that He only has good thoughts and plans for us, Jeremiah 29:11. We will then naturally be more at ease with the supernatural nature of God that we cannot seem to explain or control.

As long as we live in this fallen and darkened world, there will always be a little disconnection between us and the supernatural. We see this in many Bible accounts, telling us of people, multitudes, and even Jesus' very own disciples being amazed, trembled or in some degree of fear after witnessing some of the acts and miracles of the supernatural.

> [26] And when the disciples saw Him walking on the sea, they were troubled, saying, It is a spirit; and they cried out for fear. [27] But straightway Jesus spake unto them, saying, Be of good cheer; it is I; be not afraid, Matthew 14:26-27.
>
> And they were all amazed, and they glorified God, and were filled with fear, saying, We have seen strange things today, Luke 5:26.

Understanding the fear of the Lord

Several other accounts also tell of similar human emotions after seeing acts of the supernatural. But understand that this fear is simply man's emotional reaction to a supernatural event that they cannot logically understand and a power that they cannot control nor are comfortable with. And realize that this fearful emotion has nothing to do with the kingdom concept of walking in "the Fear of the Lord."

Points to Ponder:
Similar NT. Scriptural Concerns:

- As we apply New Testament teachings and concepts, we must always bring with us Old Testament principles if they are applicable. For, we are to build line upon line, precept upon precept, Isaiah 28:10.

- The foundation of "the fear of the Lord" is to hate evil, Proverbs 8:13. This has not changed, nor will it ever change.

- Praise God, for we can serve Him without fear. It was prophesied by Zacharias shortly before the birth of Jesus, that we would be delivered out of the hand of our enemies, that we might serve Him without fear, Luke 1:74.

Two Kingdoms, One Lawgiver:

> And Jesus went about all Galilee, teaching in their synagogues, and preaching the gospel of the kingdom, and healing all manner of sickness and all manner of disease among the people, Matthew 4:23.

We need to place a greater emphasis upon kingdoms, for we all live in a kingdom whether we acknowledge it or not. Our churches today preach a whole lot about Bible doctrine but not much about the kingdom of God. It's my belief that if we were more kingdom-focused, we would discern better between righteousness and unrighteousness. Likewise, we would also better understand Bible concepts and the principle of "the fear of the Lord."

The church today has made the concept of "the fear of the Lord" into a Bible doctrine, able to be explained apart from God's righteous kingdom. Whereby, fleeing from evil (the darkness), to then being able to live in God's kingdom of light, is a simple and fundamental kingdom concept. It is by no means an easy thing to do, nor does it come naturally, as we live on this physical earth. Even our Lord Jesus Christ in His earthly ministry, as the Son of Man, also experienced and commented on this.

Understanding the fear of the Lord

> But I have a baptism to be baptized with; and how am I <u>straitened</u> till it be accomplished! Luke 12:50.

Jesus here was talking of His death, Crucifixion and Resurrection. And how He was pressed (*in the way*), until it be accomplished." The world that we live in operates within various degrees of shades of gray; seeking the light and operating in the light is just not this fallen world's way. Thus, to again show us a visual of how narrow the way is, let's again take a look at the spectrum between light and darkness.

> [13] `Go ye in through the strait gate, because wide *is* the gate, and broad the way that is leading to the destruction, and many are those going in through it; [14] how strait *is* the gate, and compressed the way that is leading to the life, and few are those finding it! Matthew 7:14.

This scripture is speaking of living a lifestyle of abiding in the light, rather than making an initial decision to believe in Christ. For the kingdom of darkness has many shades of gray (various degrees of unrighteousness), offering enticements to please everyone. Whereas, the kingdom of light accounts for only a small sliver of pure righteousness.

Two Kingdoms, One Lawgiver:

Scripture tells us that God's kingdom is within us, Luke 17:21, yet because of man's free-will each of us chooses the level of light that we walk in. However, if we desire to find His kingdom within us, we need to be walking and abiding in the light.

There are only two types of kingdoms.

> Giving thanks unto the Father, which has made us meet to be partakers of the inheritance of the saints in light: [13] Who has delivered us from the power of darkness, and has translated *us* into the kingdom of His dear Son, Colossians 1:12-13.

Even though God has delivered us from the power of darkness, we can still choose to live there. But if we do this either knowingly or unknowingly, know that there is only one righteous Lawgiver and we shall all undergo His righteous judgment.

God, the one righteous Lawgiver:

> **There is one Lawgiver, who is able to save and to destroy: who art thou that judges another?**, James 4:12.

> But I will forewarn you whom ye shall fear: Fear Him, which after he has killed has power to cast into hell; yea, I say unto you, Fear Him, Luke 12:5, {Matthew 10:28}.

A righteous God must judge unrighteousness.

There is only one Lawgiver. God is the only person able to send you to your final destination, whether it be heaven or hell. Our adversary Satan does not have the power to send a person to hell. All he can do is to deceive you through various worldly means and keep you living an unrighteous lifestyle. Thereby causing a righteous God, at the Day of judgment to have to condemn His unrighteous creation to eternal damnation.

But, God wishes that all His people would come to the knowledge of salvation. For, hell was not made for man, but for the devil and his angels, Matthew 25:41. However, God gave man freedom of choice, and He will not override man's free-will. We can either choose to believe in Christ and claim His righteousness, or we can choose to believe in the ways of the world, thinking that we are self-sufficient and do not need Christ's salvation. Thereby leaving ourselves open to be judged unrighteous on the last day by the righteous Lawgiver.

It is our choice of where we place our fear:

It is our choice where we place our fear. We can somehow fear the righteous Lawgiver that judges us

Two Kingdoms, One Lawgiver:

to be either righteous or unrighteous, causing us to distance ourselves from Him, by setting up a fake front. Or we can learn to hate unrighteousness as much as God hates it, causing us to depart from evil, and thus being drawn even closer to Him. But no matter where we place our fearful concerns, God's judgment remains just and righteous.

Where you place your fear or concern may seem like a rather small thing, thinking it's only the end result that really matters. However, God's system is a belief system, rather than the natural based system that we are used to; and to operate in God's kingdom we must abide by His kingdom principles.

You can see how this works when you read the parable of the <u>servants entrusted with their master's money</u>. The servant that did nothing with his portion of the money was judged harshly by the master. This servant actually called his master a hard man and a thief, and he was judged accordingly. Thus, when we have even a fearful concern towards God the righteous Lawgiver, we set up a barrier between us and God and thus we also get dealt with accordingly. Thus, you can see how our thoughts and how we perceive others greatly determine how they in return deal with us and how they in return, judge us.

Understanding the fear of the Lord

The word, "fear" itself

The word "fear" can be used as either a noun or a verb.

Noun: Implying an emotion, danger or fright usually related to another person.

Verb: Implying to be afraid, frightened, dreading or anxious of a certain situation.

Even in this simple noun & verb definition, the lines are still blurred as to what actually caused and invoked the fear. However, we can see from this simple example that the word fear can cover an array of emotions, ranging from a feeling of dreading a certain situation to sensing danger or literally being afraid of a person or thing.

The concept of the fear of the Lord, I believe was better understood during the early church age, even perhaps being a fairly common and understood phrase in those days. For when Apostle Paul preached in Antioch, he stood up in their synagogue and said: "Men of Israel, and ye that fear God, give audience," Acts 13:16. If the phrase "fear God," was viewed as a negative thing, much like people think of it today, I doubt if the Apostle Paul would have used it to promote the presentation of his message of grace to the Gentiles.

Two Kingdoms, One Lawgiver:

What I propose here is that we think of the word "fear" more-of as a verb: being afraid, frightened, or even in dread of a certain inevitable situation. Such as: getting caught up in living an unrighteous lifestyle and then on the judgment day being declared unrighteous by the righteous Lawgiver.

God's thoughts on the matter:

The thought of a righteous God, who is the essence of love, having to condemn His unrighteous creation that are made in His own image to eternal damnation, must be almost unbearable for Him. There is no way around this, for a righteous God must condemn all unrighteousness; otherwise He would no longer be righteous.

This will happen to those who choose to live unrighteous lifestyles on the Day of Judgment, and tells us of dread or a fear of what the Father will be required to do on that day.

Saying this by no means removes responsibility from us. For it's always our choice whether we choose to hate and flee from evil or not and this will direct the outcome of our life. My point is that how we abide or fail to abide in the light affects not only us but also God as well.

Jesus was heard because He feared.

> Who in the days of His flesh, when He had offered up prayers and supplications with strong crying and tears unto Him that was able to save Him from death, <u>and was heard in that He feared</u>, Hebrews 5:7.

Jesus was and is 100% Man and 100% God, yet He was heard because He feared. Jesus could not have been in fear of the Father because He was also God and one with the Father, John 10:30. Yet even Jesus feared the lures and enticements of unrighteousness, for He knew that a righteous God would judge all forms of unrighteousness. This also needs to be an example for us today, as we strive to live a righteous and holy life. Thus, we should not direct our fear towards God, but rather fear living an unrighteous lifestyle.

Why such a scary name?

Or have we simply made it appear to be scary? There is no doubt that in today's times, the word "fear" gives the phrase a negative tone. Yet since "the fear of the Lord" actually means hating and fleeing from evil (the darkness), why not call it: "being a servant of righteousness" or "walking in the light."

Two Kingdoms, One Lawgiver:

These last two names don't sound scary and they don't scream, "danger or warning" at us.

I believe, God wanted to underscore the dangers of what living an unrighteous lifestyle can do to us, how it can distract us from ever seeking His Son and His salvation, therefore leading to our own eternal damnation. Perhaps figuring that it would be better if His people even had a false concept of Him, rather than to perish, being caught up in unrighteousness.

It is an age-old principle, for our good.

> The LORD commanded us to do all these statutes, <u>to fear the LORD our God</u>, **for our good always**, that He might preserve us alive, as *it is* at this day, Deuteronomy 6:24.

This scripture also applies to us today; knowing and abiding by "the fear of the Lord," is for our own good. In Old Testament times, a direct fear towards God was what the people could best understand, for they were under the law. But now as New Testament believers, having further knowledge of God's Word and kingdom. We need to leave our unrighteous ways behind us and progress in our understanding of the things of God, being able to now walk in the light as He is in the light, 1st John 1:7.

Points to Ponder:
Two Kingdoms, One Lawgiver:
- Jesus preached about the kingdom of God, and that also needs to be our focus as well. It is as simple as light versus darkness, life versus death, etc.
- The kingdom of God is within us, Luke 17:21. It is within the light, but as long as we are abiding in the darkness, we will not be able to find it.
- Choosing to hate evil and fleeing from evil will also position us to receive God's many blessings. Walking in the light, as He is in the light, 1st John 1:7, is an essential kingdom principle.
- God is the only Lawgiver, and no one will escape His righteous judgment. Therefore, choose whom you will serve.
  > Know ye not, that to whom ye yield yourselves servants to obey, his servants ye are to whom ye obey; whether of sin unto death, or of obedience unto righteousness? Romans 6:16.
- In this section, praise the Lord because He has given every man free-will to choose. We can all choose the righteous ways of His marvelous kingdom.

How scripture defines evil.

Knowing and understanding how scripture defines what evil is, shows us a way that we can achieve walking in "the fear of the Lord," rather than just knowing the biblical truth of "hating evil and fleeing from evil." Through understanding how scripture defines evil, we can begin to control our personal darkness, the evil that we partake in, and thus we can begin moving towards the light. This is how scripture defines what evil is:

> The fear of the LORD *is* to hate evil: <u>pride, and arrogancy</u>, and <u>the evil way</u>, and <u>the froward mouth</u>, do I hate, Proverbs 8:13.

Here we see four conditions of evil;
- pride
- arrogancy
- the evil way
- the froward mouth

Three of these attributes speak of conditions that are directly attributed to man's unrenewed heart, and we shall also see that "the evil way" is also about heart issues. Note: that none of these address what we might think as being overt sinful actions, and that is because the Lord is much more interested in the thoughts and beliefs of man's heart and mind.

Understanding the fear of the Lord

The evils of pride.

Pride: Inordinate self-esteem; an unreasonable conceit of one's own superiority. – *Webster's Dictionary.*

Let's first take a look at scriptures concerning man's pride and how God sees it.

In the Old Testament the Lord told the Israelites, if they would not hearken to Him, He would break the pride of their power, Leviticus 26:19. God smites and is against the proud, Psalm 12:3, 31:23, 101:5, Proverbs 15:25, Isaiah 25:11 & Jeremiah 50:31. God respects not the proud, Psalm 40:4. Pride is as a chain about your neck, Psalm 73:6, The Lord rebukes the proud, Psalm 119:21, and He only knows the proud from afar, Psalm 138:6. Shame comes through pride, Proverbs 11:2. In the mouth of the foolish *is* a rod of pride, Proverbs 14:3. All those who are proud in heart are an abomination to the Lord, Proverbs 16:5. Pride is the first step to destruction, Proverbs 16:18, and man's self-pride will deceive thee, Jeremiah 49:16 & Obadiah 1:3.

Jesus also spoke about man's self-pride and He categorized pride as being that: which defiles a man, Mark 7:22. John writes of all that is in the world, the lust of the flesh, and the lust of the eyes, and the

How scripture defines evil.

pride of life, which is not of the Father, 1ˢᵗ John 2:16. In the Epistles, man's pride is spoken of as an evil attribute, Mark 7:22, Romans 1:30. In the last days, men will become proud, 2ⁿᵈ Timothy 3:2. God has scattered the proud, Luke 1:51 and God resists the proud, James 4:6 & 1ˢᵗ Peter 5:5.

All of these scriptures make it clear that God hates man's pride, because pride will possibly keep man from ever seeking Him and receiving all the blessing of His salvation. Self-pride is perhaps man's greatest downfalls, allowing one to think that they are self-sufficient and a bit superior to others and able to do it all on their own

The world teaches us self-pride from the day we are born. From the prideful 5-year-old telling his parents that he will do it himself, to the adult that feels they need to put letters before or after their name to let others know of their high social status or their great accomplishments.

Although pride may be an ongoing temptation in this physical life, 1ˢᵗ John 2:16, it is always our choice if we wish to become proud or to create a habit of walking humbly. For scripture tells us that it is when we think of ourselves as more highly than we ought, Romans 12:3, it becomes our downfall.

Understanding the fear of the Lord

And whosoever shall exalt himself shall be abased; and he that shall humble himself shall be exalted, Matthew 23:12.

Pride *goes* before destruction, and an haughty spirit before a fall, Proverbs 16:18.

Pride is always destructive; there is no such thing as a good pride. It is destructive to the person speaking it, and can also cause negative results or pressures to be put on the person receiving the boastful affirmation.

Throughout the scriptures, God never refers to His workmanship in a prideful manner. In Genesis, during creation, God called the heavens, the earth and His creation as being *"very good."* Later in the New Testament, it is recorded that God was *"well pleased,"* with His Son Jesus, Matthew 3:17, Mark 1:11, Luke 3:22 & 2nd Peter 1:17.

The antidote to pride is having a grounded and confident relationship with the Lord. For pride in its most basic form is thinking of yourself as your own god. And the only way to break this is to be fully confident and dependent on the Lord, able to rest assured in your relationship with the Lord. Only then will we find it easy to attribute the abilities that He has blessed us with back to the Lord.

How scripture defines evil.

The world has turned most type of pride into a good thing. Pride in yourself to be able to go it alone, and feel good about yourself. This is not at all how God intended it to be; we are once again calling what is evil – good, and good – evil. For God intended for us to be dependent on Him and each other.

Pride may initially boost up our ego making us feel that we are superior to our fellow man or holier than the rest. However, pride will eventually bring us to our own demise. For when we approach God, through our self-pride, He generally steps back and leaves us to our own self-efforts and this always destines us for a fall; it's just a matter of time.

The evils of arrogancy:

> **Arrogancy**: Overbearing pride evidenced by a superior manner toward inferiors. – *Princeton Online Dictionary.*

Arrogancy and pride go together, where pride is the internal condition of the heart, arrogancy is the outward expression of a prideful heart. Simply put: it is man's self-pride spoken in a boastful way exalting oneself over others. We clearly see this in the parable that Jesus gave to us of the Pharisee and the Publican in, Luke 10:9-14.

Understanding the fear of the Lord

In the parable, both men went up to the temple to pray. The Pharisee not only trusted in himself, his own works and keeping his tithes (pride), but he also exalted himself over the other man, praying within himself (arrogancy). Whereas, the Publican did neither of these, but rather humbled himself.

Let's also look at the instances of how and when the word "arrogancey" was used in scripture.

- When Hanna dedicated the child Samuel to the Lord, she prayed a general caution not to allow arrogancy to come out of thy mouth, 1st Samuel 2:1.
- Isaiah prophesies that the arrogance of the proud shall cease, Isaiah 13:11.
- Jeremiah prophesies about the arrogance and pride of the people of Moab, Jeremiah 48:29.

The world walks a fine line on this one too, of always letting others know of your talents and abilities, but at the same time discouraging ultra egos. Arrogancy takes pride to an even deeper conviction, by speaking it over and over until this boastful mindset becomes your lifestyle.

This is not the way of the Lord for mankind, for He wishes for all men to live humbly and in peace with each other, Romans 12:18.

How scripture defines evil.

The evil way

Most of us would consider this alone to be evil because it appears to be dealing with external situations or actions rather than issues of the heart, but as we look at this in greater depth, we will see that it is also speaking of heart issues.

Jesus defined the "evil way" as being pretty much synonymous with the ways of the world.

> The world cannot hate you; but Me it hates, because I testify of it, that the works thereof are evil, John 7:7.

Perhaps we can better understand this by realizing "the evil way," is to make use of only natural resources apart from God's supernatural provisions. For the world's way of operation, is to handle all issues through relying on man's intellect and natural resources. For the natural world has no belief in God's Word or His supernatural provisions.

In this physical world we have a spiritual enemy, John 10:10, and many spiritual forces come against us. This enemy and thief comes to us with various forms of deception and oppression, wanting us to believe that our answer only lies in working within the natural realm, that he has dominion over.

Understanding the fear of the Lord

If we fall for this lie, we have not only chosen the "evil way" or the natural way, but we have also committed ourselves to worldly defeat. For the only way we are going to become victorious in this natural world is to take up and use the weapons of warfare that Christ has made available to us.

> **For the weapons of our warfare** *are* **not carnal, but mighty through God to the pulling down of strong holds;** 2nd Corinthians 10:4.

The only way that we can overcome this natural world is to pray without ceasing, and to use His spiritual weapons to overcome the natural ways of the world.

Thus, the extent to which we walk in the evil way is dependent on our belief or you could say lack of belief in God's Word. We might think of man's free-will as only applying to our decision for Christ, (choosing life eternal over everlasting damnation); however, it is ultimately up to us as to what degree we believe in God's powerful Word.

We can believe greatly in His Word or we can mix in degrees of the natural way in with it. Thus, what we believe, our personal philosophy will ultimately determine the degree to which we walk in the evil way.

How scripture defines evil.

The evils of the froward mouth:

Froward: habitually disposed to disobedience and opposition.

In the days of Middle English, froward was also defined as: "moving or facing away from something or someone:" – *Merriam Webster Online Dictionary.*

They that are of a froward heart *are* abomination to the LORD: but *such as are* upright in *their* way *are* His delight, Proverbs 11:20.

God called the Israelites in the desert a froward generation, Deuteronomy 32:20, and in Psalms and Proverbs we see the froward compared to the wicked, the evil, the crooked, the perverse, those that sow strife, and all that are froward are an abomination to God, Proverbs 3:32, 11:20.

Other words from the dictionary that apply are: headstrong and self-willed, improper, in rebellion and difficult to deal with. Whereas the definition over the years has remained much the same. I recommend that we give thought to the earlier definition of: "turning away from something or someone," suggesting that the froward person has turned away from the Word of truth and from God Himself.

The antidote is of course to be obedient to God, we can either do this the easy way or the hard way. We can either willingly choose to be submissive, or we can dwell in our stubbornness until we become broken. Knowing that whosoever shall exalt himself shall be abased; and he that shall humble himself shall be exalted, Matthew 23:12. God most always get His way; therefore, I recommend that you pick the first option.

In Conclusion:

What the Lord considers to be evil has to do with the thoughts of man's unrenewed heart. Pride is an internal matter of the heart, and arrogance is an outward boasting of a prideful heart. The evil way is how much of the natural ways of the world we adopt as opposed to believing in God's Word and His supernatural provision. The froward mouth refers to the rebellious, those that refuse to be obedient to God's Word and ways but rather are headstrong set on stubbornly pursuing their own wicked and lustful desires.

The good news is that we can control all of these, for every man has control over his own thoughts and beliefs. This is also a function of man's free-will; we

How scripture defines evil.

can choose what we think and believe. By doing this we can start controlling our personal inner darkness that we dwell in. We might not even see these four attributes as dark things or evil attributes; however God sees it this way.

This is great news because whereas it is impossible to control the darkness within the world, all we need to control is our own inner darkness, our thoughts and beliefs and we can all do this if we but have the desire to do so.

Scripture tells us that we are able to take every thought captive (evaluate), and cast down (reject), the dark thoughts, 2nd Corinthians 10:5. This makes this teaching very practical as we can control our own personal darkness and evil thoughts that we allow ourselves to partake in.

To start this process of having mastery over our thoughts and thus our behavior. We not only need to use certain spiritual tools, but we also need to possess wisdom and understanding which is an essential key to the kingdom. In the next section, we will address all of this further and how we can limit or even eliminate the darkness from our lives.

Understanding the fear of the Lord

Points to Ponder:
How scripture defines evil.

- What the Lord calls evil are the thoughts of the unrenewed heart; (<u>pride</u>, <u>arrogance</u>, <u>the evil way</u> and <u>the froward mouth</u>).
- These four attributes all originate from the heart, and we ultimately have control over what we allow our mind to think and meditate on.
- Our thoughts, if left unchecked over time will impregnate themselves on us and direct our steps. Therefore, decide today what you believe and will partake in, the kingdoms and unrighteous ways of this fallen world or the righteous ways of the kingdom of the living God.
- Praise the Lord because He will give us a new heart and a new spirit, Ezekiel 36:26, and we have the mind of Christ 2nd Corinthians 5:17. He has given us all that we need to overcome negative thoughts if we desire to do so.

Our thoughts matter the most.

For as he thinks in his heart, so *is* **he: . . . ,**
Proverbs 23:7.

Our thoughts are important! Through right thoughts, all the blessings of the kingdom of God will be opened unto us, for our thoughts and desires are what directs it all. Ultimately our thoughts dictate to us who we are and direct our destiny and we become as we think. In other words, our thoughts and the words that we speak mold and shape us.

We have seen down throughout history that as the beliefs of people have changed entire nations have been changed. Two examples are the Berlin wall and Germany during Hitler's reign; one was a change for the better and the other for the worse.

Propaganda works! Bringing this closer to home, television commercials work. If this were not the case, companies would not spend hundreds or thousands of dollars for a 15-second advertisement slot. What we see and hear plants thoughts in our mind and those thoughts influence us. To either buy the product or not. Likewise, we are also influenced by the message of the television program that we may simply see as entertainment.

Understanding the fear of the Lord

Controlling our thoughts is required if we wish to progress and be victorious in our Christian walk. For the Lord's way of operating is a belief system as opposed to the world's natural system of seeing and then believing. Rather God's way is by calling things forth that are not as though they were, thus, believing and then seeing it manifest, Romans 4:17.

> For verily I say unto you, That whosoever shall [23] say unto this mountain, Be thou removed, and be thou cast into the sea; and shall not doubt in his heart, but shall believe that those things which he saith shall come to pass; he shall have whatsoever he saith [24] Therefore I say unto you, What things soever ye desire, when ye pray, <u>believe that ye receive *them*, and ye shall have *them*</u>, Mark 11:23-24.

The mountain here in this scripture is the obstacle or the problem that we need to deal with. God's system is solely dependent on what you believe and speak. For these verses do not talk of having the needed resources, the money or the skill, rather they talk about speaking what we desire in prayer and believing that we will receive it. Therefore, we should consider it quite natural to be able to control our thoughts and likewise cast down negative thoughts.

Our thoughts matter the most.

We all must control our thoughts.

For we become as our thoughts direct us. The thoughts and philosophies that we entertain and believe in, whether they be right or wrong only become stronger and more ingrained throughout our lives. We have also seen such to be true where if you repeat a lie or a form of reasoning long enough, you will begin to believe it to be true. Thus, before thoughts form a stronghold in our mind, we need to take every thought captive and cast down (reject), the thoughts that do not promote righteousness.

> **Casting down imaginations, and every high thing that exalteth itself against the knowledge of God, and bringing into captivity every thought to the obedience of Christ,** 2nd Corinthians 10:5.

Casting down thoughts and imaginations is not just for the super saints, nor is it just an academic exercise, this is something that all believers must do. God would have been unjust to give us a command to take control of our thoughts if it were impossible or if only a select group of people could do so. In fact, everyone that wishes to live the Christian life and achieve the promised abundant life must be able to control their thoughts.

Either we will control our thoughts or our thoughts will control us.

> And be not conformed to this world: but be ye transformed by the renewing of your mind, that ye may prove what *is* that good, and acceptable, and perfect, will of God, Romans 12:2.

> For to be carnally minded *is* death; but to be spiritually minded *is* life and peace, Romans 8:6.

Here, we are talking of more than just our common salvation of getting up to heaven and having eternal life with Christ. Understand that to have the fullness of the inheritance and blessings that Jesus secured for us through His death on the cross and Resurrection operating in our life, we must abide within Him. This may sound very elementary but the way we do this is not through lip-service or confession, rather we do this by operating out of the mind of Christ.

> For who has known the mind of the Lord, that he may instruct Him? But we have the mind of Christ, 2nd Corinthians 2:16.

Even though we live in this physical world where sin is all around us and the world wishes to lure us into being conformed with its dark ways. We can

Our thoughts matter the most.

partake of the light of God's Word, for it's not about the physical kingdom we abide in; it's about our thoughts, what we believe and adhere to. Through the new birth and now being new creatures in Christ, we can strive to operate out of the mind of Christ and our thoughts and desires can become pure and righteous, rather than thinking that we must operate from the mind-set of the world.

Thus, to flee the darkness or the vices of the world, we do not need to become a monk or a nun; we do not need to escape up to a mountain so as to live in solitude, away from the evils of the world. Rather we simply need to renew our mind so that all of the dark and unrighteous thoughts are gone.

Thus, we can control our inner darkness.

Controlling our thoughts allows us to control and minimize or eradicate our own personal inward darkness. This is important because scripture as we saw in the last section, defines evil to be the thoughts of man's unrenewed heart. Therefore, if we can control our thoughts and transform our mind with the reading and believing of God's Word, we can flee from evil, thus allowing us to abide in "the fear of the Lord."

Another benefit of doing this is that you will now be walking in the light, as He is in the light. Likewise, the fullness of Christ's inheritance and His many blessing are also open for us to receive.

> But if we walk in the light, as He is in the light, we have fellowship one with another, and the blood of Jesus Christ His Son cleanses us from all sin, 1ˢᵗ John 1:7.

> Blessed *be* the God and Father of our Lord Jesus Christ, who has blessed us with all spiritual blessings in heavenly *places* in Christ: Ephesians 1:3.

Beginning steps on controlling your thoughts:

First, we must realize that we need the help of God's Holy Spirit to do this. For the world's system will never teach us the ways of righteousness and peace, nor will it happen through our intellect or our own will-power. For this is a fallen world and everything in it is also fallen. Thus, everything around us has been tainted and our carnal mind (of the 5-senses) has only dark, corrupted and less than righteous data to work with.

Second, we must have a strong desire to take control and clean up our thought process; if we have this desire and the willingness to do whatever it

Our thoughts matter the most.

takes, I believe we are more than halfway there, and that God will gladly assist us in the process.

Third, we must know that not every thought that we have is ours. What I mean by this is that we have an enemy in this world and his main weapon is deception (that has to do with one's thoughts). Our thoughts generally come from three sources; they can be thoughts from God, thoughts from our own intellect or from the world's system, or thoughts directly from the devil and his demons.

In this brief example, we are going to address thoughts that we are pretty sure are dark; thoughts that we know do not contain the righteousness of Christ. When we finally realize and classify a thought as being dark and unrighteous, it should then be relatively easy and even natural to cast it down. Thus, when a dark unrighteous thought comes to you, do not own it and then condemn yourself for thinking it, rather realize that it is not your own thought and cast it down, i.e. reject it and refuse to meditate or entertain thoughts such as that.

The hurdle that we all need to get over, as stated earlier, is to mark the thought as being negative in our mind. For our old man and unrenewed mind sees nothing wrong with worldly thoughts and even enjoys and encourages them. Therefore, we must first renew our mind, by the washing of the Word.

To be successful at doing this, we will need scripture to stand on, for we cannot do this merely from our own will-power. Here I give you two scriptures to get you started on your journey;

> So God created man in His *own* image, in the image of God created He him; male and female created He them, Genesis 1:27.

We are sons and daughters of God made in His image; this is a truth that will never change! Evolution is a lie; for more information on this, read my paper on creation. As dirty as we may get or think we are, we will always be made in His image. When the prodigal son returned to his Father, he was treated as a son, for he always was a son.

> For who has known the mind of the Lord, that he may instruct Him? But we have the mind of Christ, 1st Corinthians 2:16.

We have the mind of Christ! Now we may not always be operating out of it, but as born-again believers in Christ, we have the ability to do so.

After these two scriptures have become resonate within you, it will then become easy and almost natural to cast down dark thoughts.

Our thoughts matter the most.

Learning to enjoy the many benefits of walking in the light:

> But if we walk in the light, as He is in the light, we have fellowship one with another, and the blood of Jesus Christ His Son cleanses us from all sin, 1ˢᵗ John 1:7.

> Thou wilt keep *him* in perfect peace, *whose* mind *is* stayed *on Thee:* because he trusts in Thee, Isaiah 26:3

Walking in the light *(with Him)*, as He is in the light, may not seem to be as exciting of having the immediate gratification and glitter of what the world can offer us. However, God's righteous ways are higher than our ways and they bring us into perfect peace, joy, and fulfillment, giving us eternal life.

There are several benefits to walking in the light, as He is in the light and all of us can do this. For the kingdom is within each and every believer, Luke 17:21, and God is no respecter of persons.

- We can stop looking over our shoulder to see if we have been found out yet.
- The burden that we carry through this life will be gone or greatly reduced.
- It brings personal integrity, knowing that you have done the right thing.
- We reduce our level of fear and increase our level of peace.

Understanding the fear of the Lord

- We start the journey of perfecting holiness in relationship with Him.
- We can walk in and minister in greater power and authority of God.

Points to Ponder:
Our thoughts matter the most.
- It is all about our thoughts and desires; as a man thinks in his heart so is he, Proverbs 23:7.
- We are a new creature, old things have passed away, all have become new, 2nd Corinthians 5:17. This includes your past ways of wrong thinking, therefore, push on to the high calling of God, Philippians 3:13-14.
- We can all take control of our own thoughts, 2nd Corinthians 10:5.
- Know that either you will control your thoughts or your thoughts will control you.
- All of us must transform our minds to the renewing of the Word, Romans 12:2. Renewing your mind is a process, don't give up!
- In this section, praise the Lord because it is all about changing our thoughts to align up with God's righteous thoughts. And all of us can do this!

Closing Comments.

"The fear of the Lord" is simply to hate evil, Proverbs 8:13. This is an essential kingdom principle that everybody needs to be aware of and follow, (believers and unbelievers alike). For we both live in this fallen and darkened world and the result is that the darkness (evil) will harm us.

The darkness will first harm us by stealing our blessings that God has planned for all of His people, and the extreme harm that it may cause is to lead us astray from ever receiving our salvation. For if we do not learn to hate evil, the darkness of this world will prevail over us and we will find ourselves beaten down and immersed within the darkness. Thus, we will not seek the righteous ways of the Lord nor will we grow in our relationship and walk in the light, as He is in the light, 1st John 1:7.

Within this teaching, scripture has shown us two areas where fear may be applied, and not abiding by the first will bring upon the result of the second.

The fear of the LORD *is* **to hate evil:** ....
Proverbs 8:13.

By not heeding this scripture to learn to hate evil (the darkness), and flee from evil. If we consider it to

Understanding the fear of the Lord

be of little concern to partake of the world's darkness and its unrighteous deeds. This leaves us open to being found living an unrighteous lifestyle and at a greater risk of God judging us to be unrighteous.

> But I will forewarn you whom ye shall fear: Fear Him, which after he has killed has power to cast into hell; yea, I say unto you, Fear Him, Luke 12:5.

For there is only one Lawgiver, and He will judge and condemn all unrighteousness. Therefore, learn to hate and flee from evil, confessing Christ, Romans 10:9, that we may live in His righteousness.

We then learned the scriptural definition of what evil was, and realized that we can control our own personal darkness, through controlling our own thoughts. Casting down the thoughts that exalt themselves against the knowledge of God, 2nd Corinthians 10:5. Thus, allowing us to then start walking in the light and growing in wisdom and understanding.

Even though we live in this darkened world, we can still partake of the light, for it's a matter of what kingdom we partake of and believe in. We do not need to depart from the world, ie. living on a mountain top seeking solitude from the evils of the

Closing Comments.

world. For walking in the light first starts with renewing your mind, through the washing of the Word, Ephesians 5:26.

However, desiring to walk in the light has to be a personal choice; it will not happen by osmosis nor will the world ever force you into it. But, know that there are great benefits to walking in the light. Therefore, I urge you brethren to make every effort to walk in the light, which is also synonymous with walking in "the fear of the Lord."

> Having therefore these promises, dearly beloved, let us cleanse ourselves from all filthiness of the flesh and spirit, <u>perfecting holiness</u> in <u>the fear of God</u>, 2nd Corinthians 7:1

This scripture was written to the church at Corinth, (a very worldly and carnal church). Therefore, all of us can renew our minds and perfect holiness, if it is our desire to do so.

Take the challenge, study it for yourself.

I realize as simple and straightforward as this kingdom concept is, it goes against the traditional teachings of reverential-fear and awe. If you are yet under this belief, I challenge you to prove it to yourself through the scriptures.

Understanding the fear of the Lord

Throughout this book I have been very comprehensive, not hiding anything. The points presented were proven throughout scriptures, rather than man's vain philosophies. And they have not shown this concept to be anything other than to hate evil and flee from evil. For fear of becoming caught-up in unrighteousness and then being pronounced unrighteous by the One righteous Lawgiver.

Because of man's free-will, all of us have the freedom to believe as we think best. And even once we become born-again believers in Christ, unless we are open to the Holy Spirits leading, God still won't direct our thoughts according to how we are to believe in His powerful and magnificent Word. Every believer has the same Word, yet it remains our choice as to how we wish to believe in it. Therefore, if you believe in some traditional teaching that you have been told, without having biblical proof of it. I challenge you, for your sake to prove out what you believe through the scriptures.

I pray that the teaching in this book will enable you to abide with Him in the light, 1st John 1:7.

If this book has been a blessing to you,
please consider writing a book review
Thank you.

Other books by the author

Journey to Healing and Wholeness

Through Correct Philosophies and Right Thinking

This book is available as a paper book or an eBook. It is written as a practical healing journey, and not just as an academia book on healing. Guiding the reader through the Word of God in a logical progression of steps, making the reader aware of the power behind the Word; for Jesus came to give us life and life more abundantly.

God's Word is able to meet all of our needs if we let His Word work in our lives. The Word can heal us both emotionally and physically, bringing us into a closer and a deeper relationship with Him.

This book addresses many relevant topics in everyday language concerning God's Word. There are over forty short and concise chapter topics that makes for easy reading.

Healing is promised to us; the determining factor is, what are we expecting from God, (little or much)? I believe that this book will increase your understanding and exception of God's Word.

Other books by the author

Parables of the Bible
Discovering the Mysteries of God's Kingdom

This book is available as a paper book, eBook and as an audiobook. It contains thirty-five unique parables that Jesus gave to us, plus a few of His short sayings, that are also marked as parables.

Jesus started His ministry by giving us the parable of new ways and old ways, then the principle of sowing and reaping. Followed by teaching parables and kingdom parables, and ending with prophetic and warning parables. Each parable is presented in a clear way, having a concise summary after it. Thus, trying not to detract from the spoken parable, but rather allowing the reader to meditate further on the truth of the parable.

The book shows you the importance of understanding the parables, for prophecy tells us that if we understand them, we would then be converted and healed. This by itself should be ample reason to desire to understand the parables of the Bible.

Other books by the author

Healing and Miracles of the Bible

Revealing the Many Ways of Becoming Healed and Whole

This book is available as a paper book or an eBook. It contains approximately forty unique healings from the Gospels and twelve healings within the book of Acts. Each one showing us different principles of healing, having a short critique after each one.

Throughout Jesus' ministry, He did both individual healings and healings of the multitudes. Each healing was uniquely done; not any two were the same. The book also tells of the healings within the book of Acts that were done by various disciples, letting us know that healing can be performed by other men.

As you read through these healings, I believe that your faith and expectancy will come alive, and you will be one step closer to receiving your divine healing.

When we truly seek first His kingdom and His righteousness, Matthew 6:33, we will have no need to seek yet another kingdom. For the kingdom of God will provide all of our needs.

You can contact the ministry through the website
PowerMinistries.info

THE KINGDOM OF GOD IS NOT IN WORD BUT IN POWER
1st Corinthians 4:20

PowerMinistries.info

Partnering with the Alpha & Omega

www.ingramcontent.com/pod-product-compliance
Lightning Source LLC
Chambersburg PA
CBHW052110070526
44584CB00017B/2427